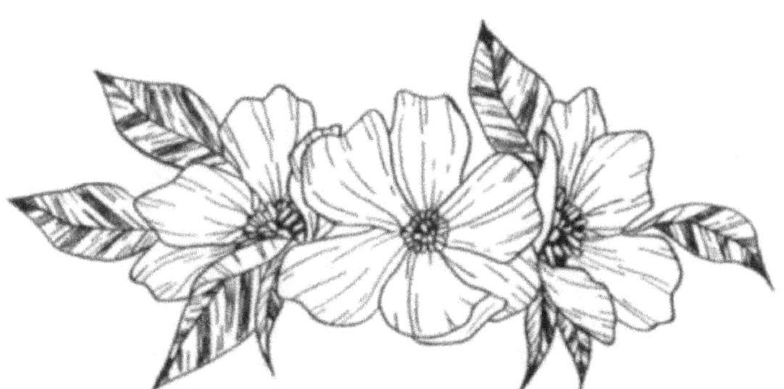

This book belongs to

....

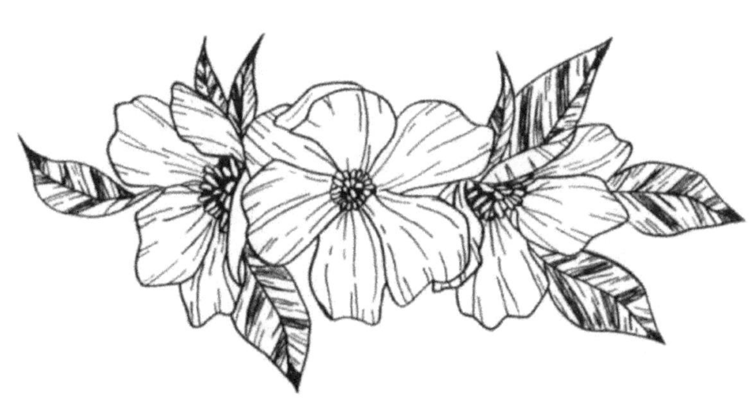

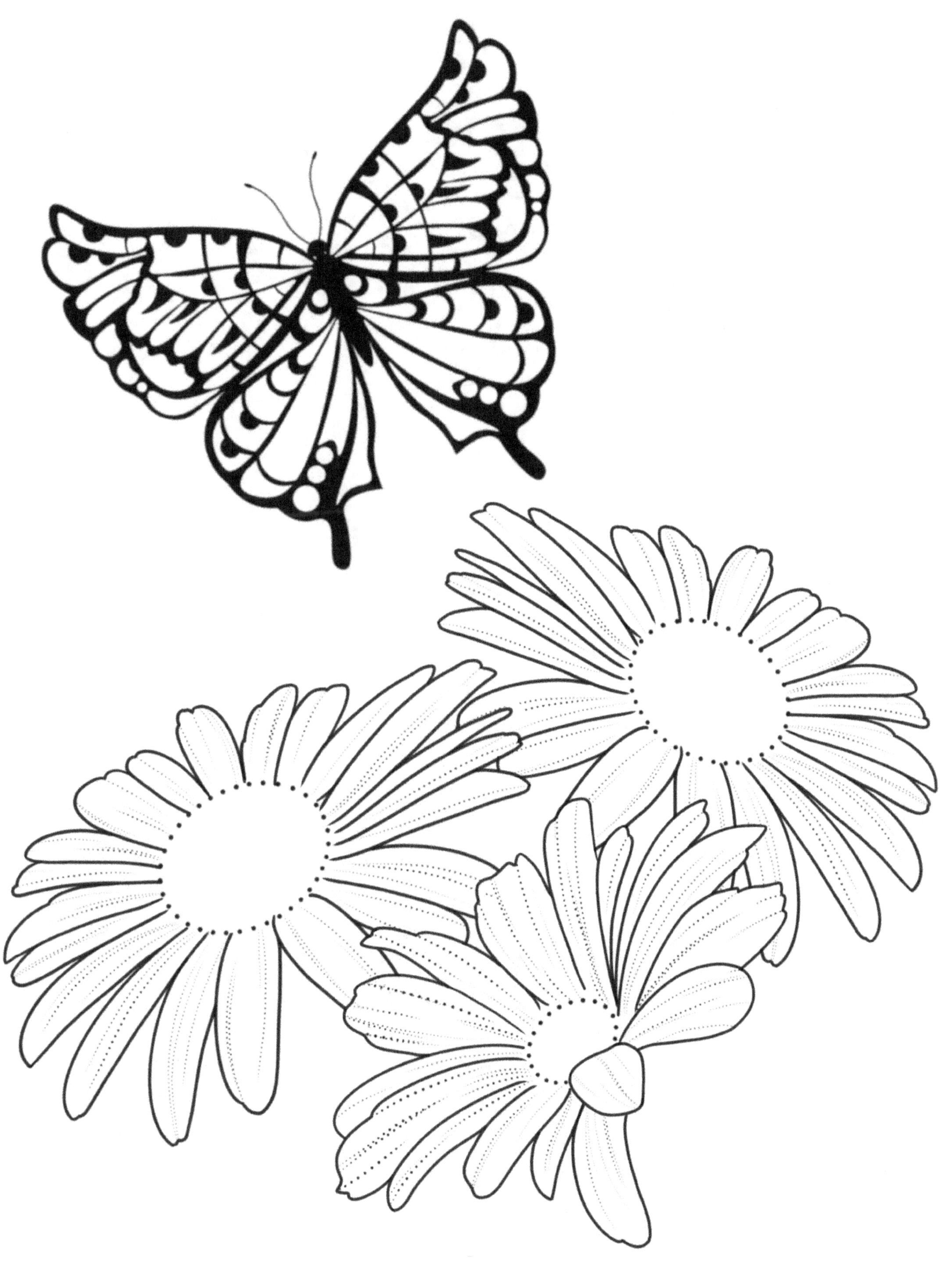

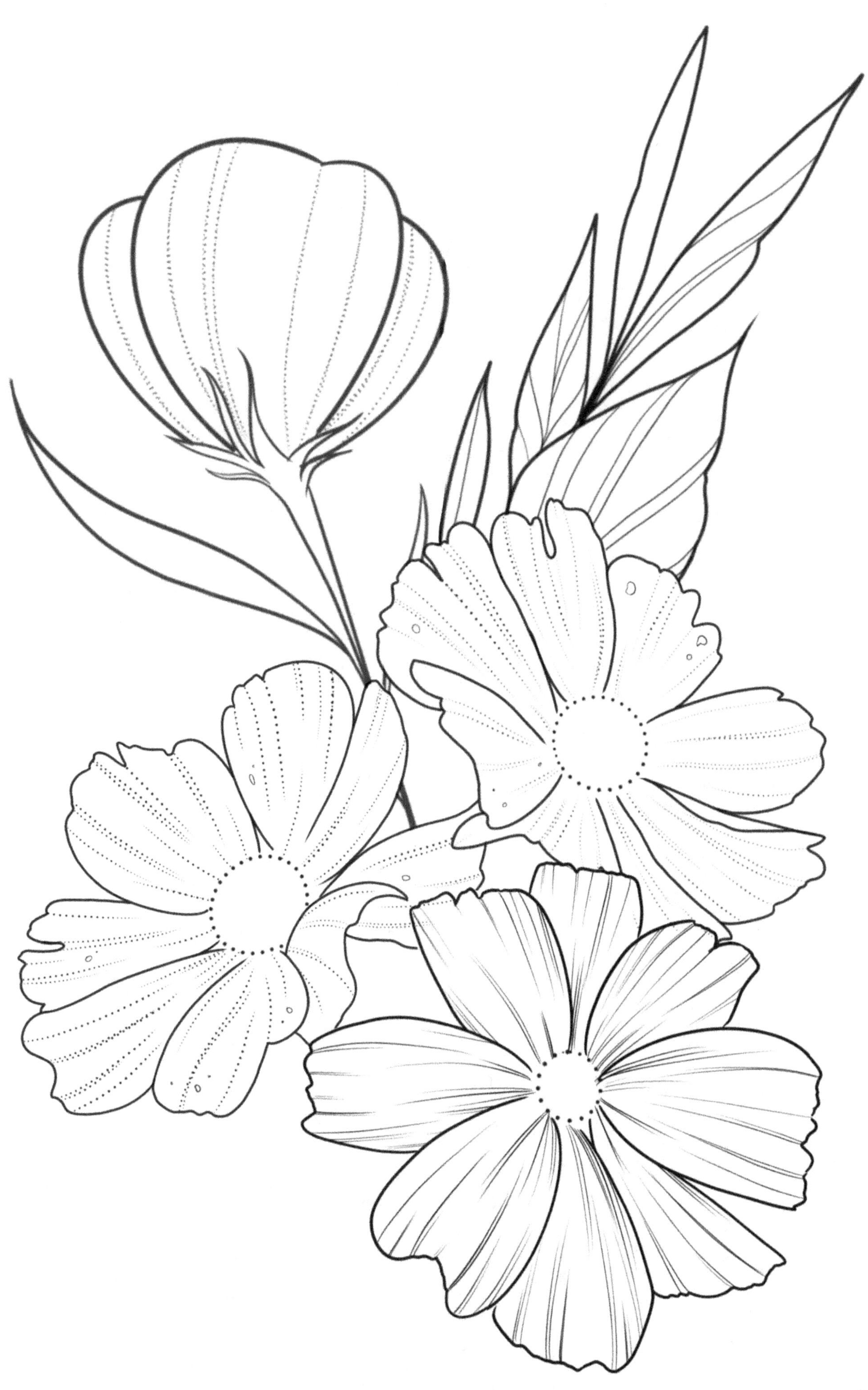

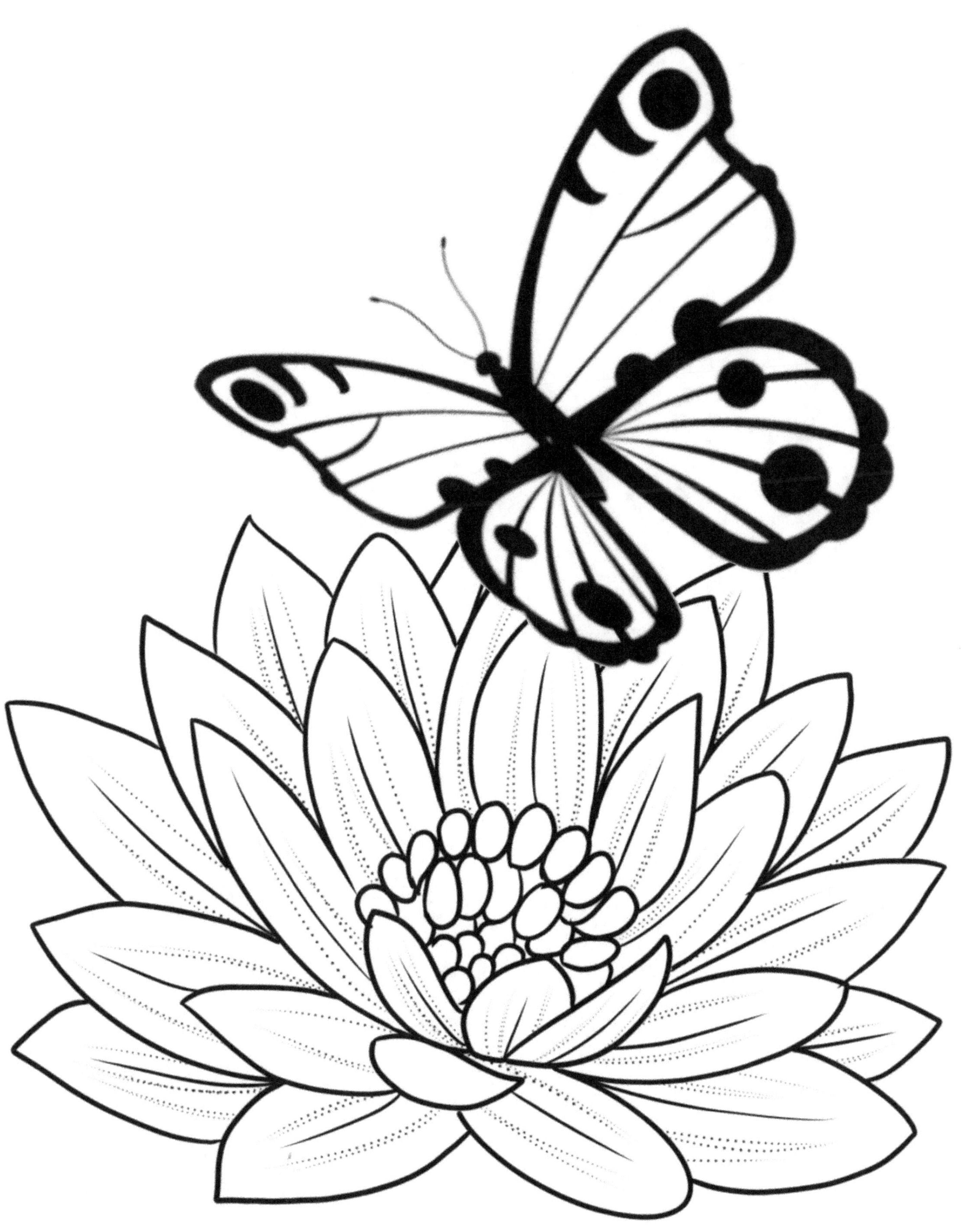

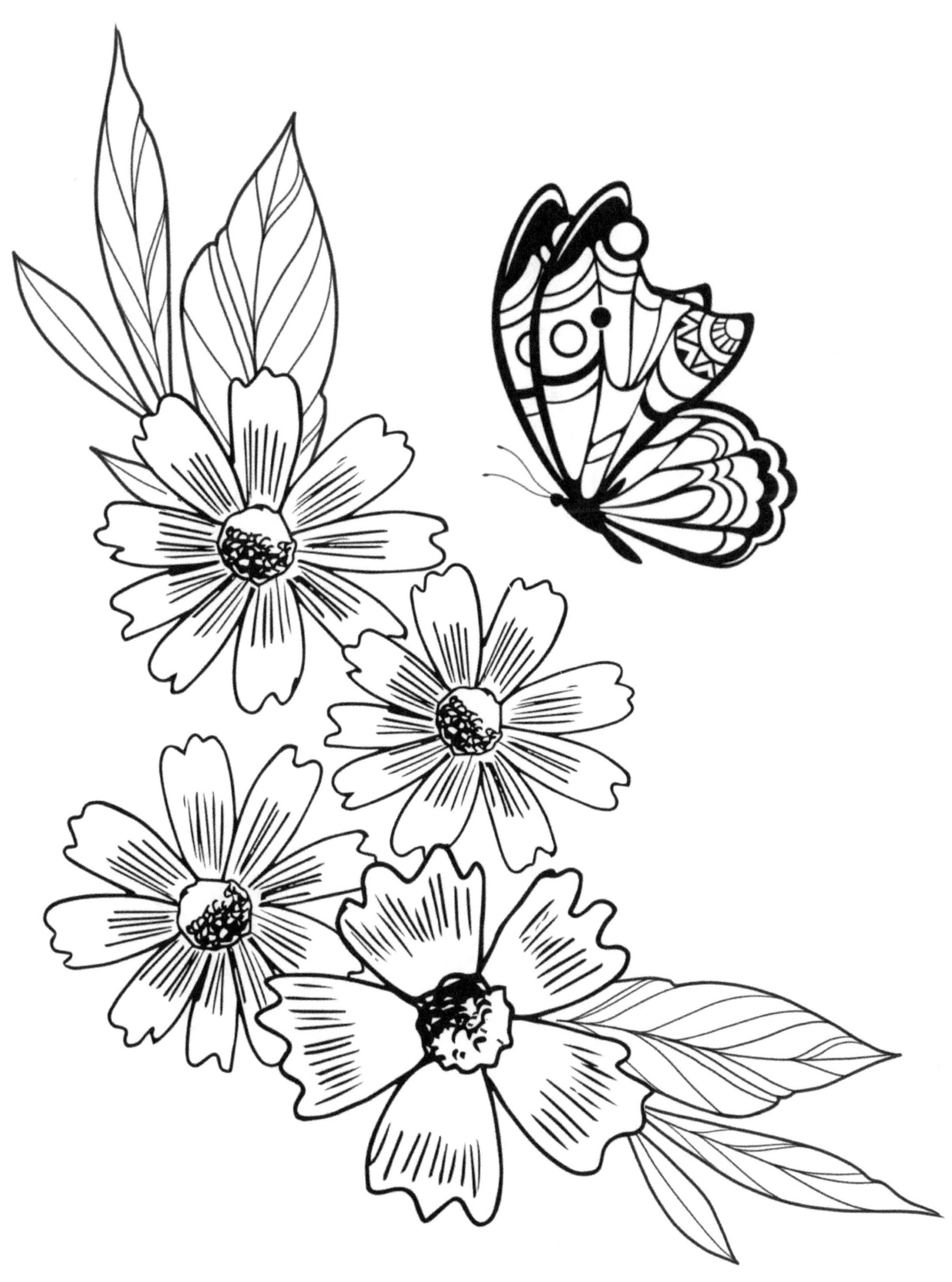

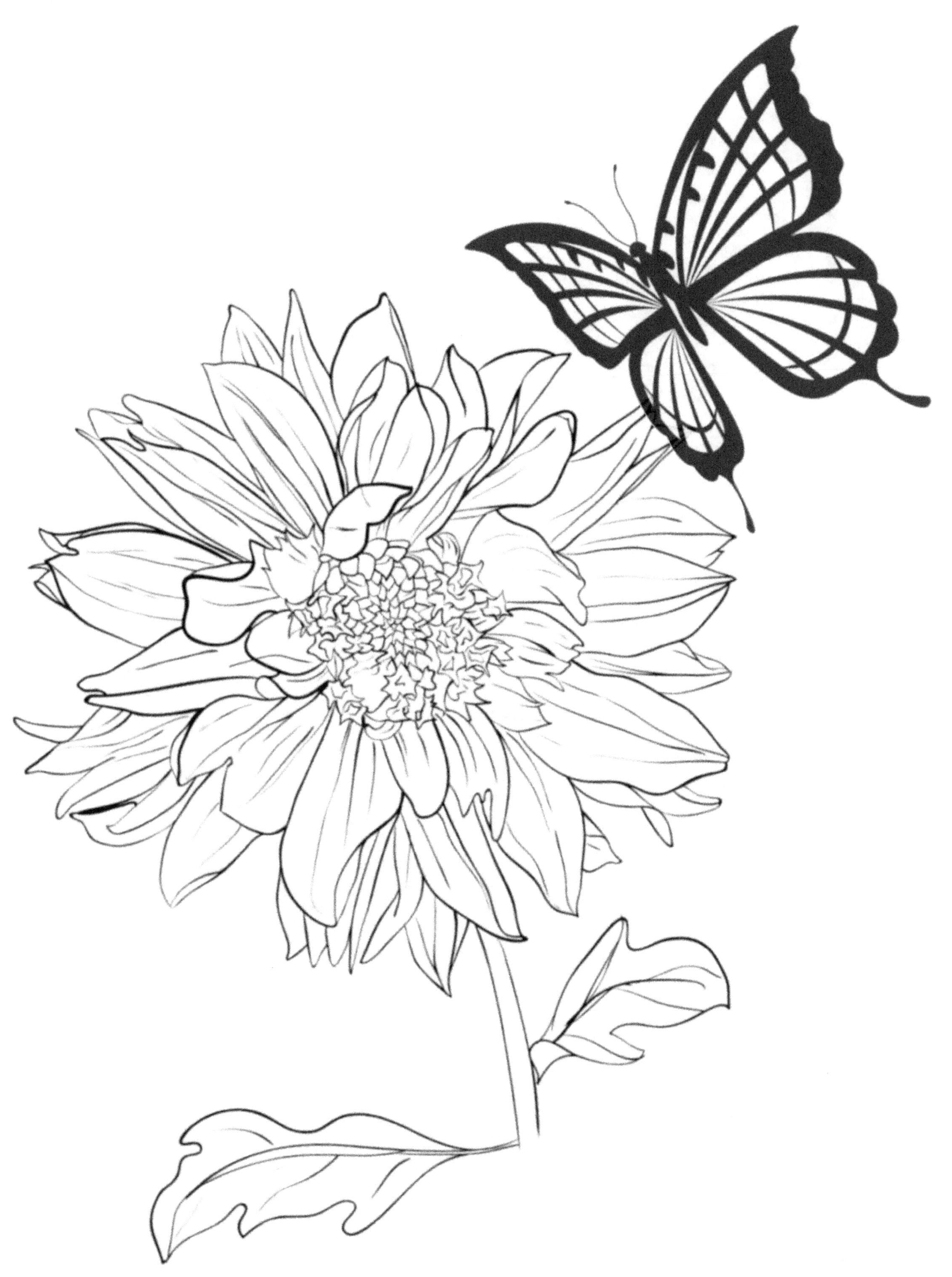

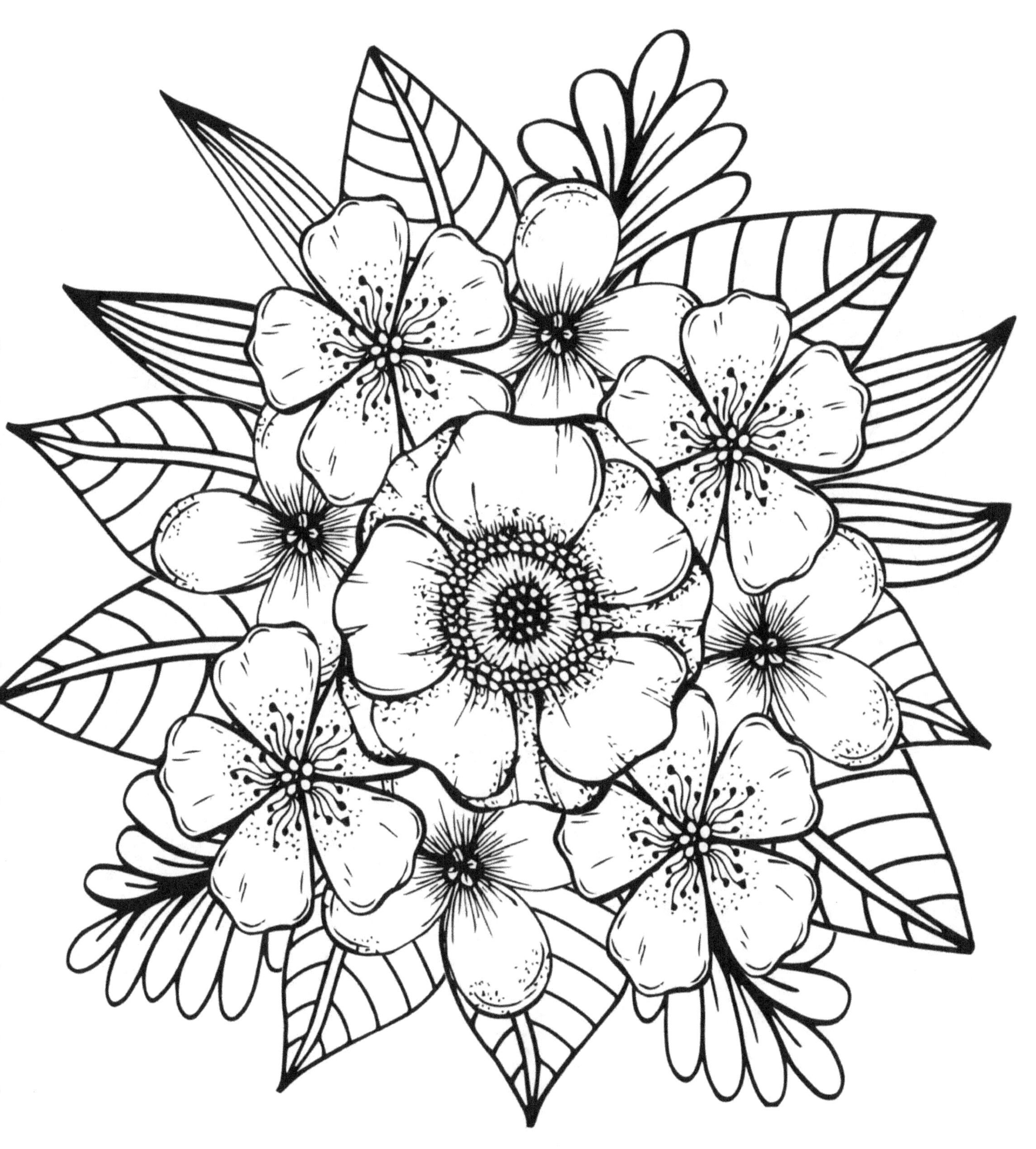

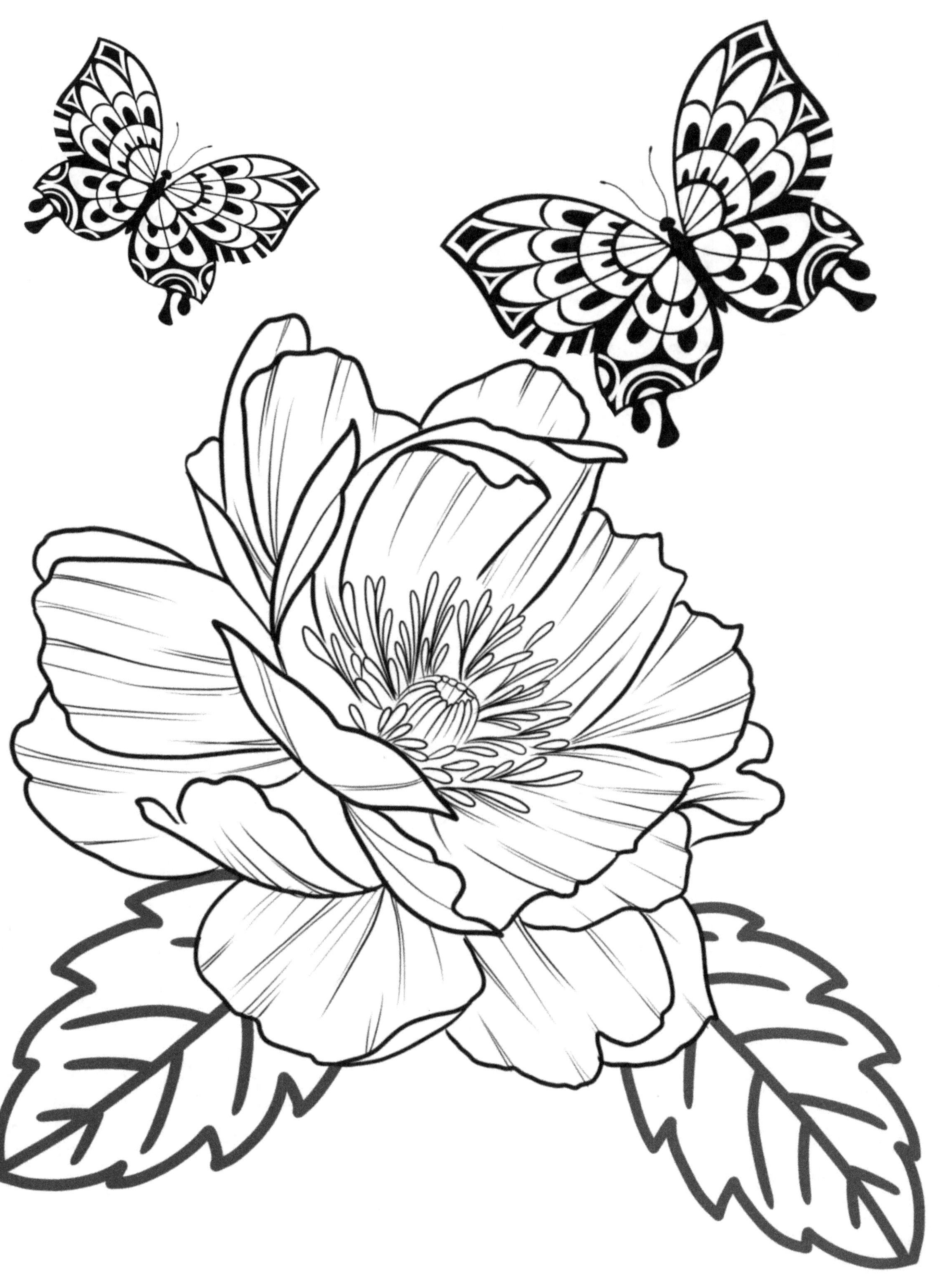

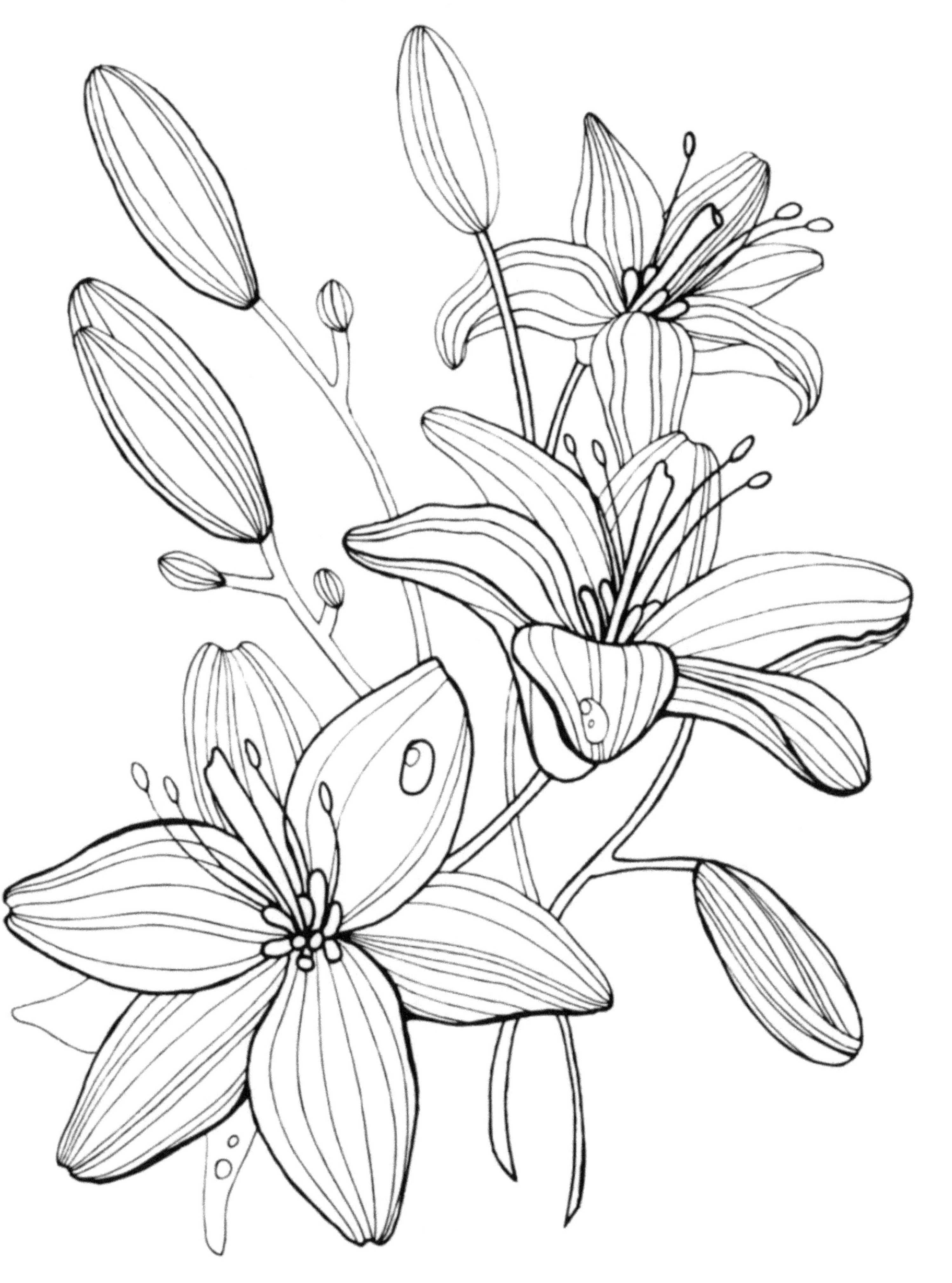

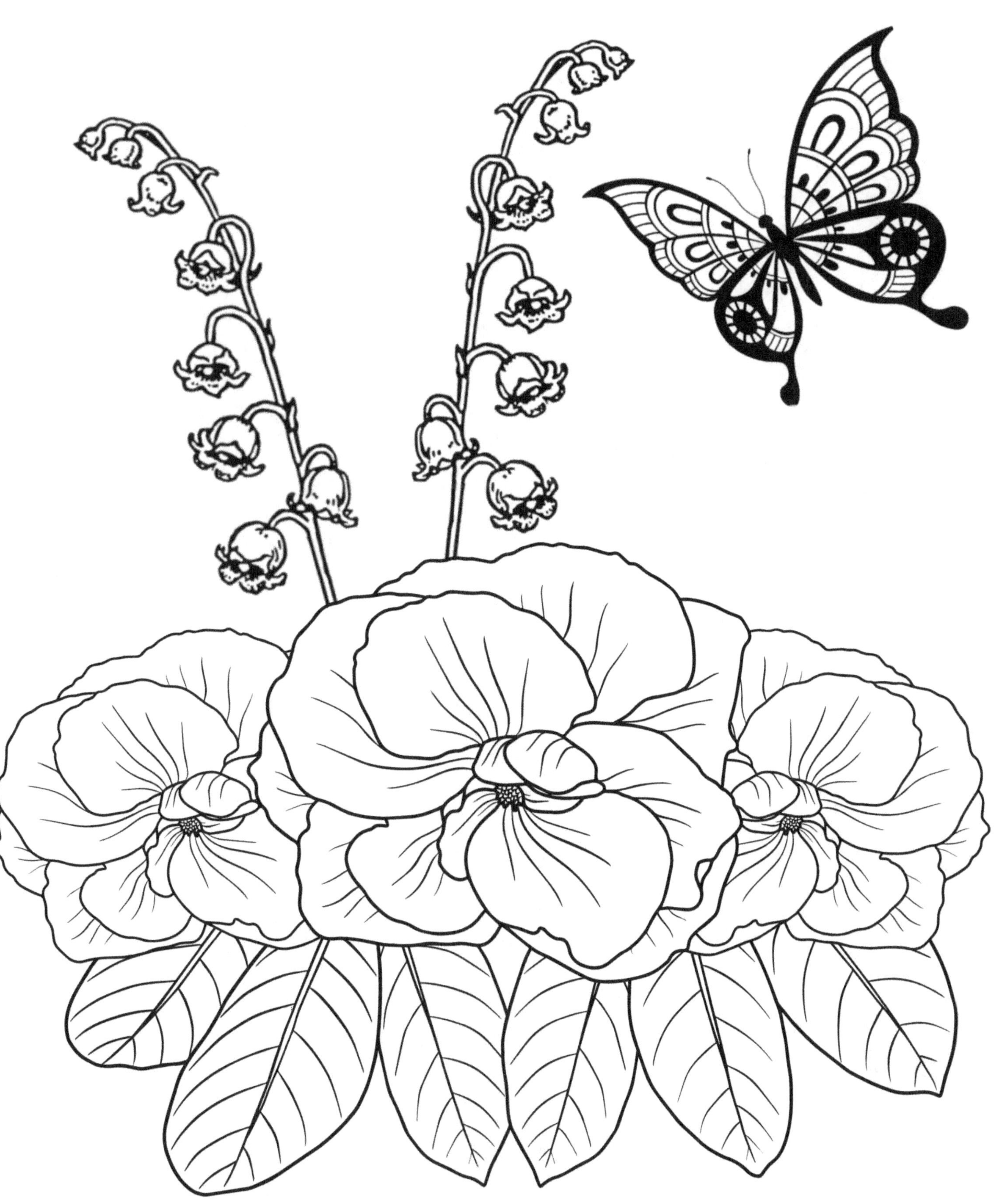

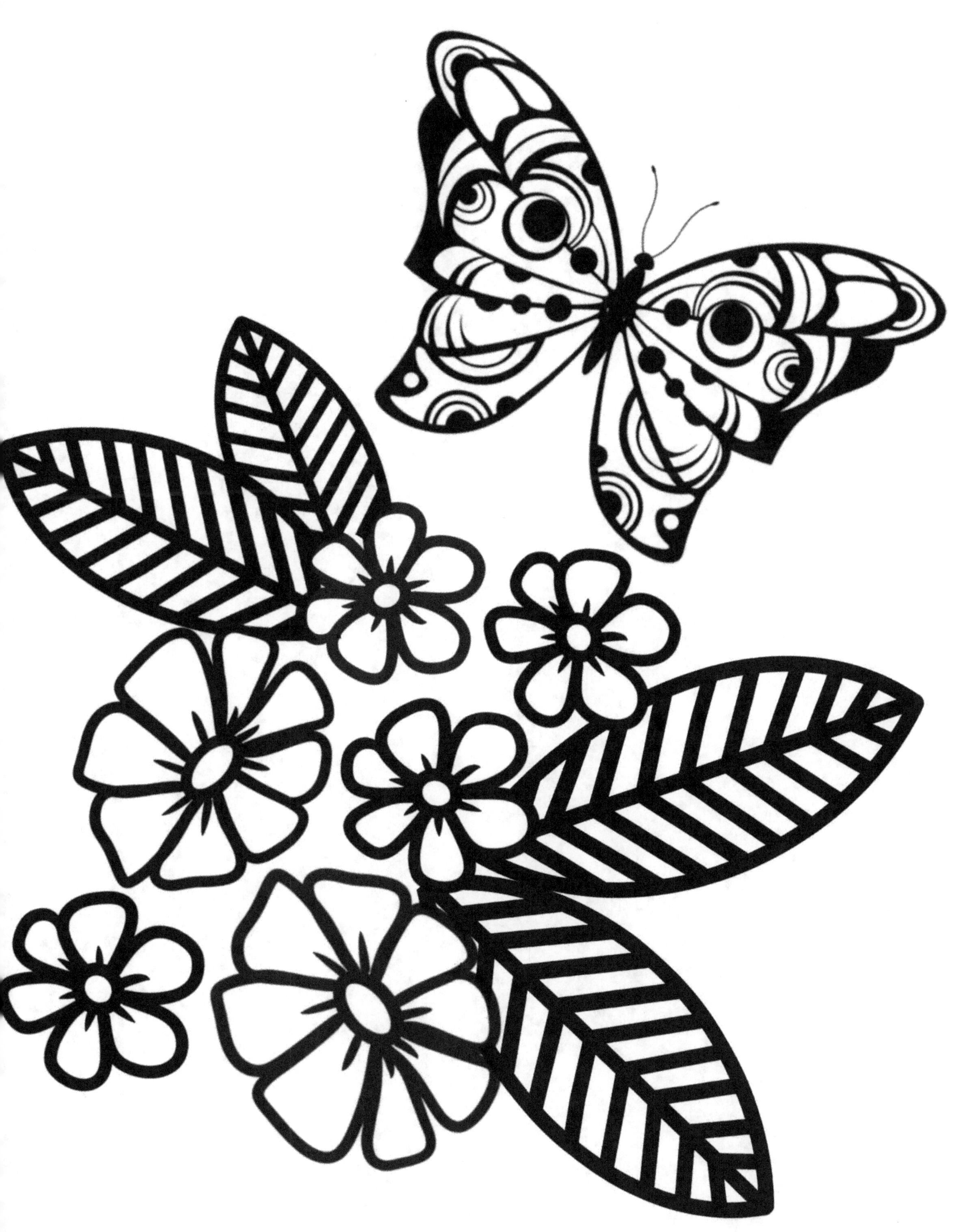

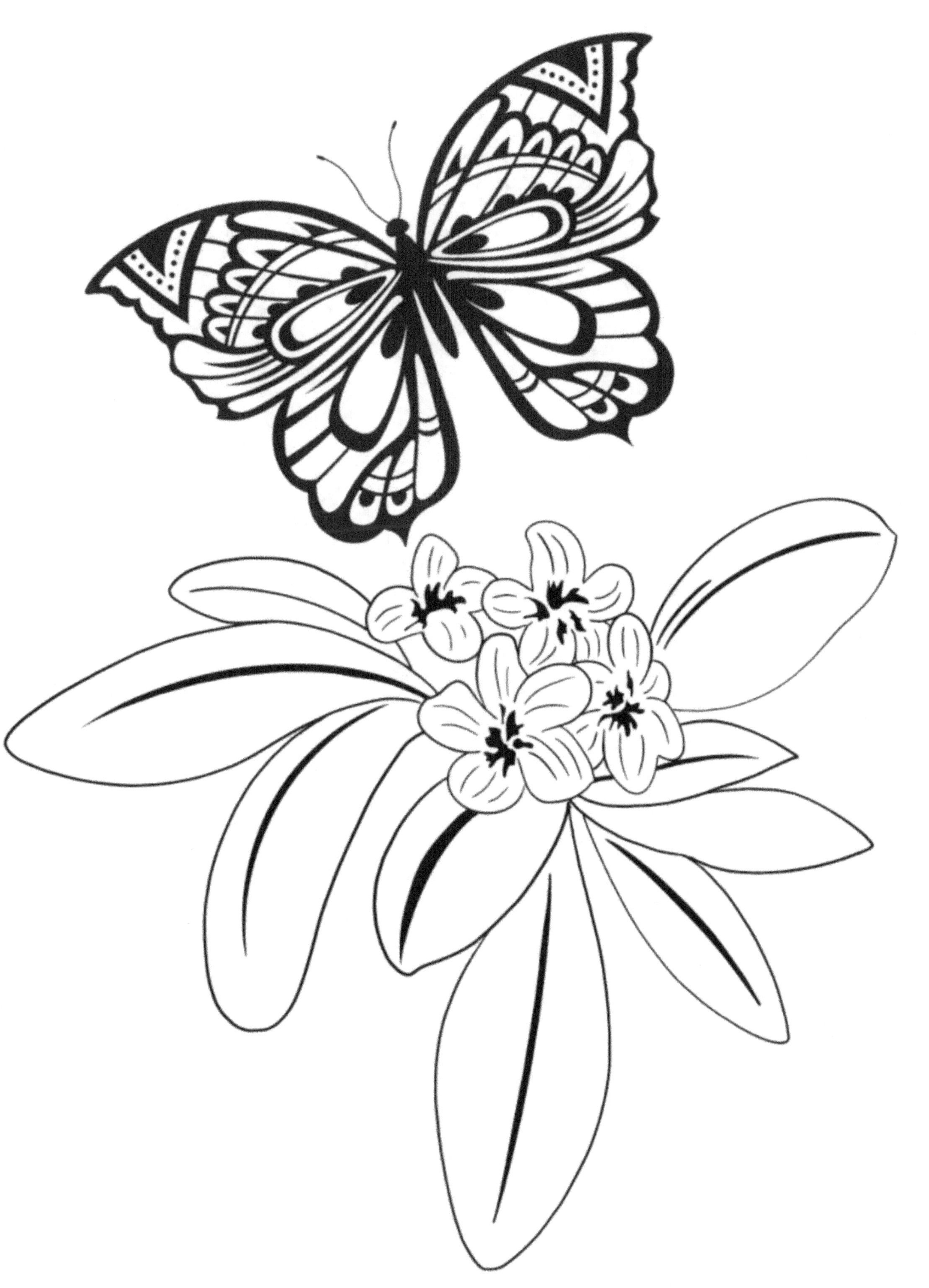

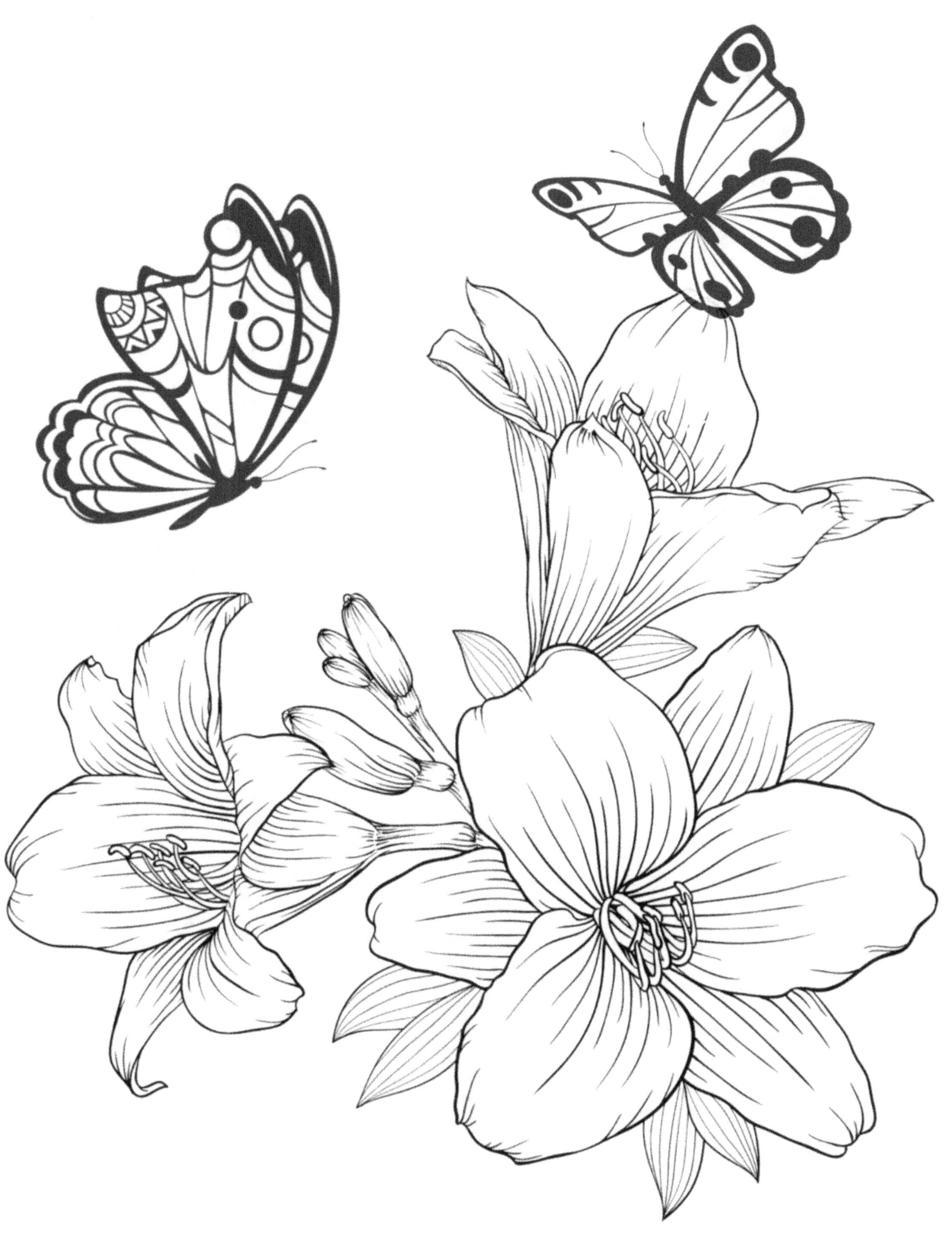

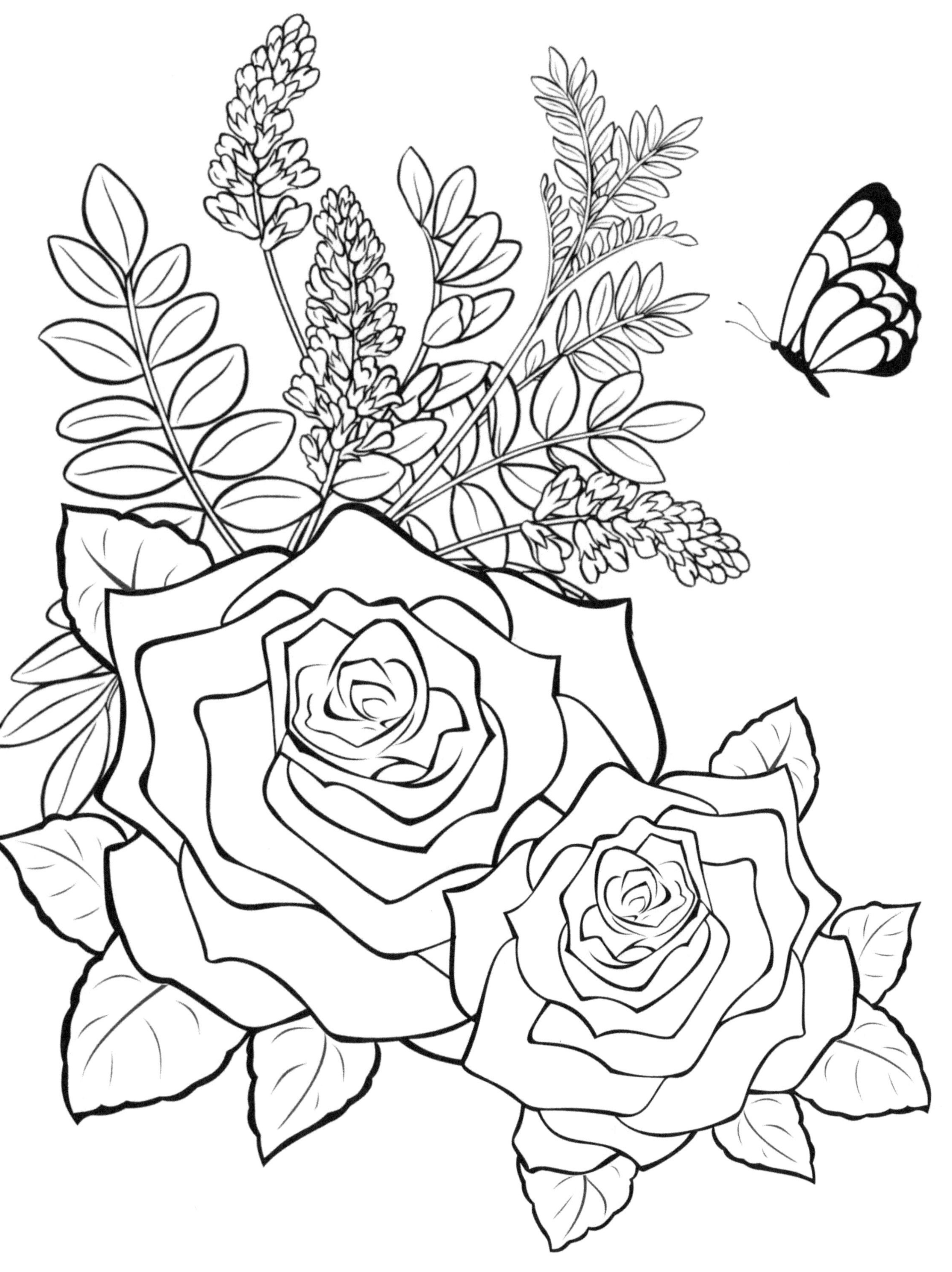

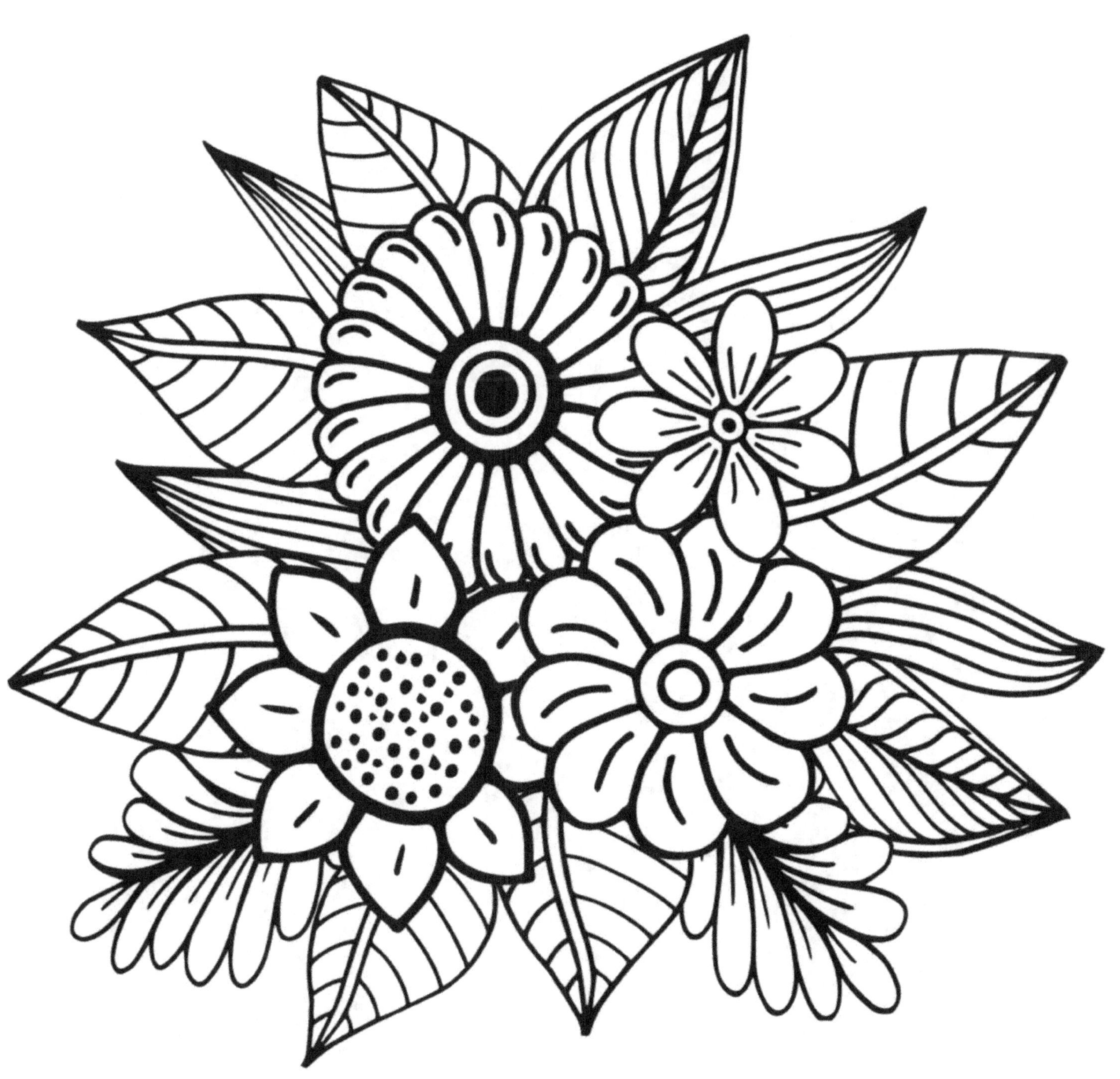

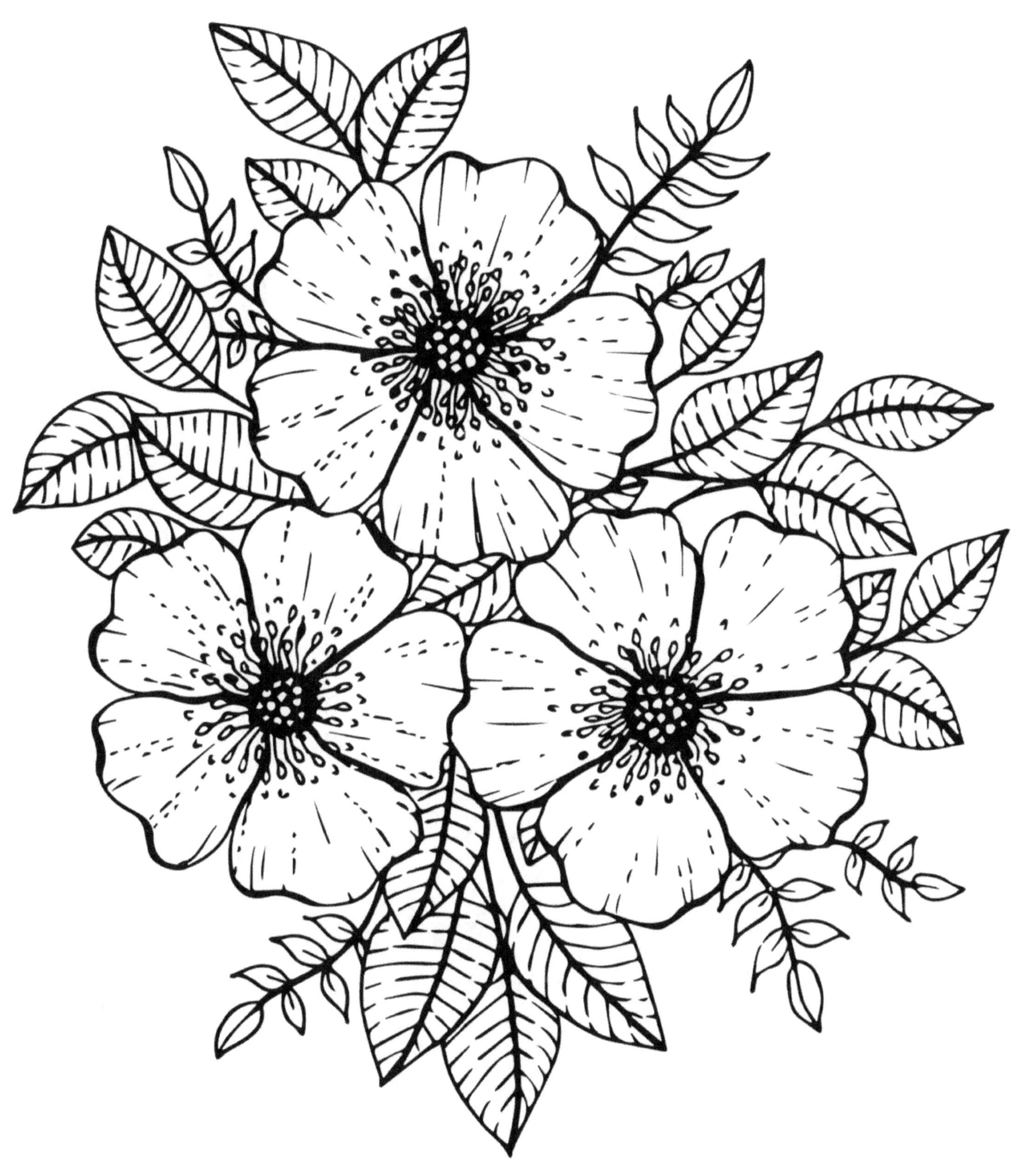

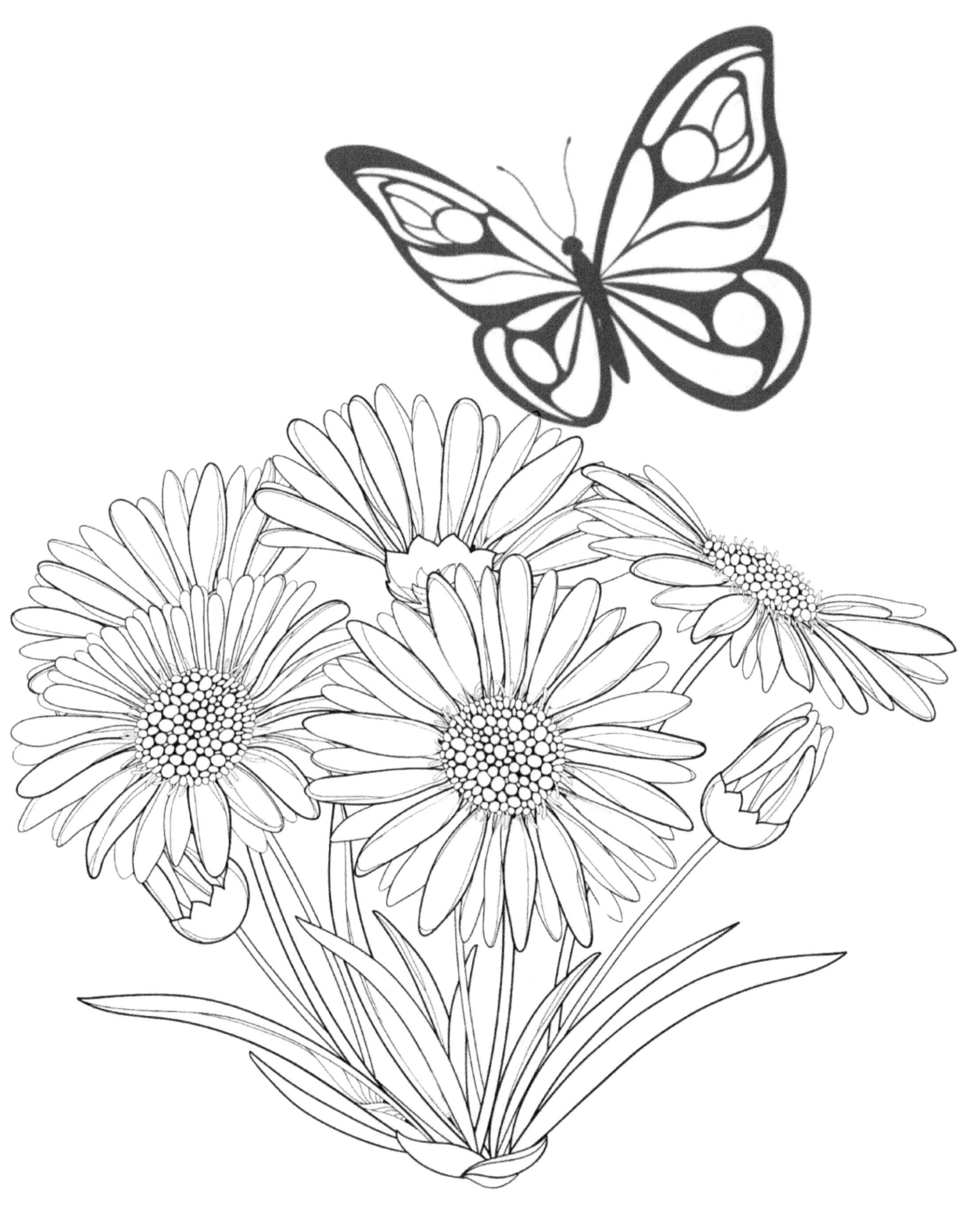

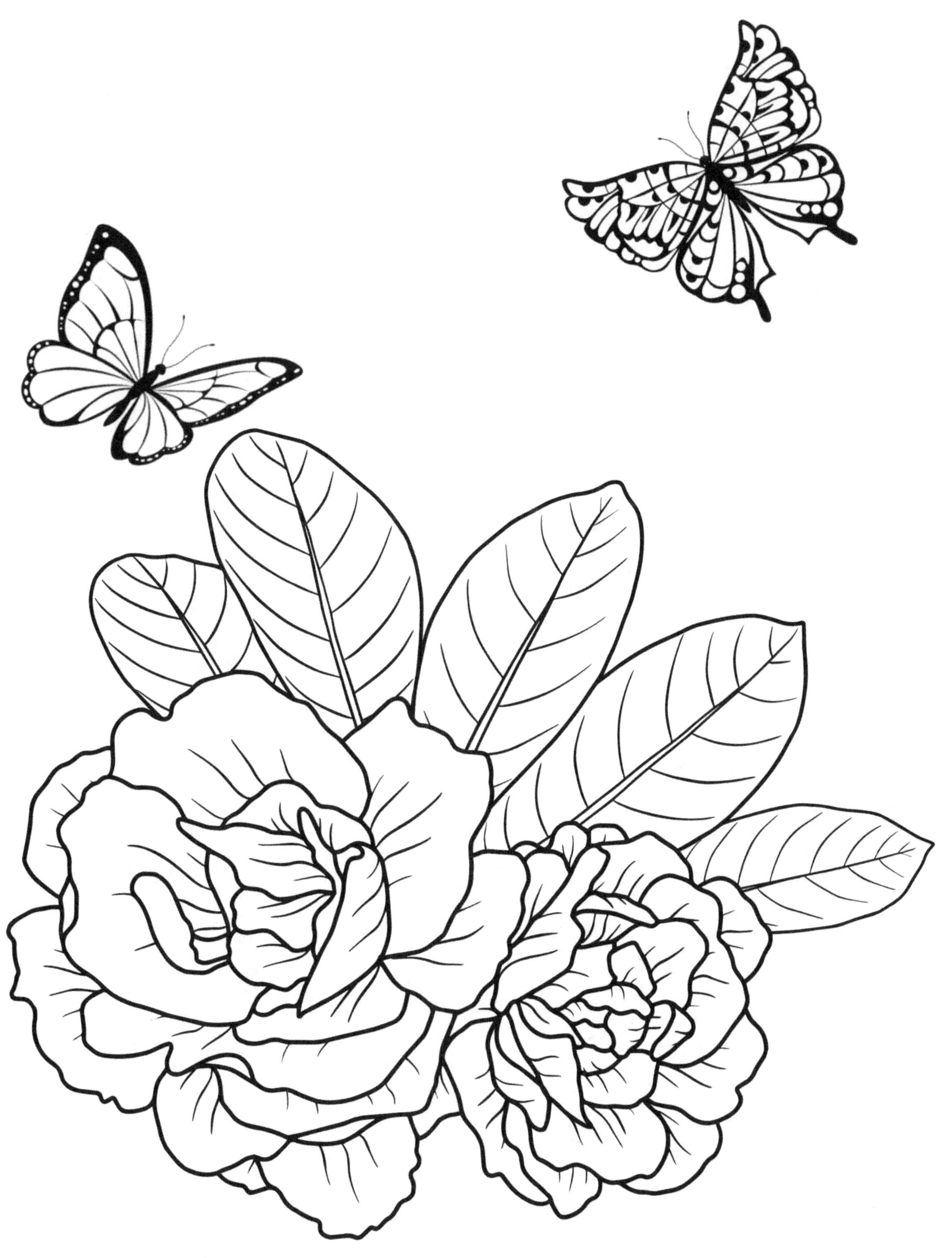

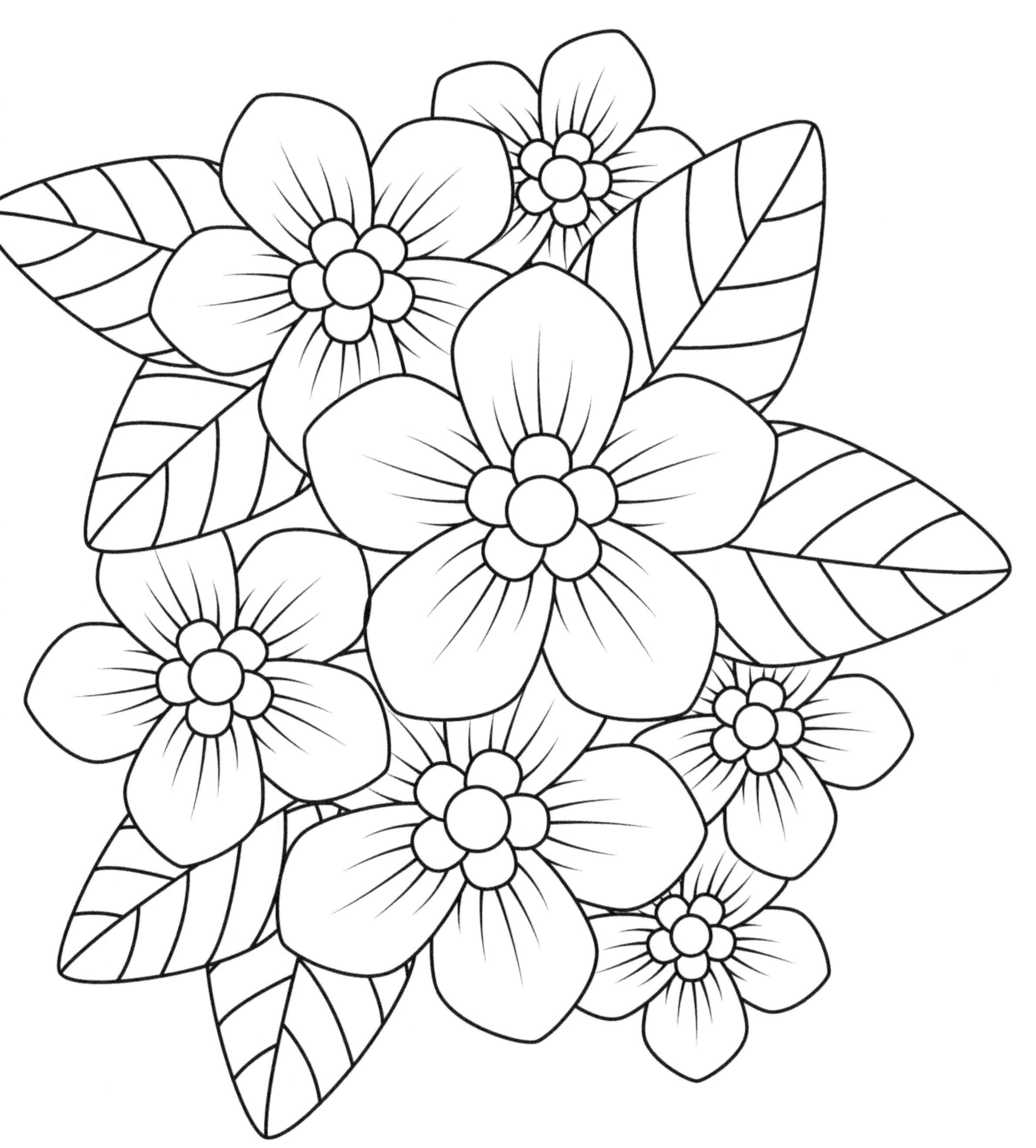

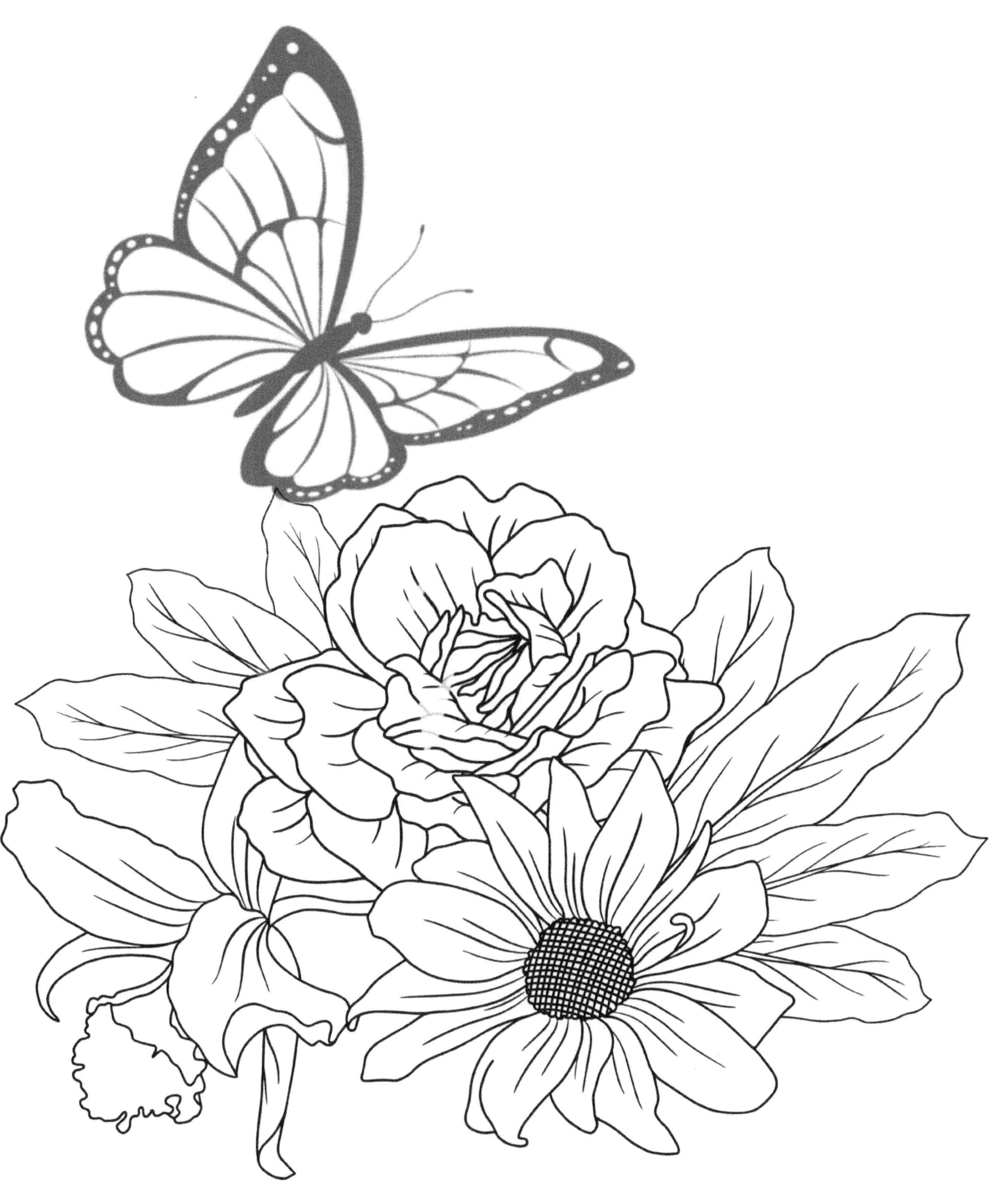